Issued under the authority of t
(Fire and Emergency Planning

Manual
Firemanship

A supplement

The Behaviour of Fire

Compartment Fires

London : HMSO

ISBN 0 11 341132 4

Preface

In 1992, the CFBAC Joint Committee on Fire Brigade Operations requested a study into what was known about flashovers and backdraughts, and the Fire Experimental Unit of the Home Office Fire Research and Development Group undertook the work. Their conclusions suggest that, whilst there are a number of areas where more research would be of benefit, a significant problem appears to be a lack of effective communication between fire scientists and the fire service, to enable firefighters to have benefit of the knowledge that is available.

This document attempts to address what firefighters need to know about compartment fires. It tries to summarise, without going into theory, what is understood about the early stages in the growth of a fire in a compartment, leading to a flashover and possibly backdraught, and the effect of ventilation. If readers want a more theoretical explanation, they should refer to text books. A brief bibliography is given at the back of this supplement.

The definitions of Backdraught and Flashover in this document are based on the state of knowledge in 1995, rather than British Standard 4422:1987.

This publication supplements Books 1 and 11 of the Manual of Firemanship and will, in due course, be incorporated therein.

The Home Office is indebted to all those who have helped in the preparation of this work.

Contents

Chapter 1
The Fire

1 Combustion

When a candle burns, the wax melts. The liquid is drawn up the wick, where it turns into a flammable vapour. It is this vapour which burns, forming the flame.

In the same way, in a fire in a compartment, it is useful to think of all the combustible materials (the fuel) as being sources of flammable gases. These gases, which need not necessarily ignite, are generated when the fuel is heated. Initially the gases result from the boiling off and decomposition (pyrolysation) of hydrocarbons, such as the resin in wood. Eventually, if they get hot enough, the remaining solids, such as charcoal in the case of wood, will themselves start to burn.

These gases rise in a plume (Figure 1.1), and mix with air. If the gas/air mixture is correct, any given ignition source (eg a flame or spark) will trigger the combustion process which will rapidly become self-sustaining. The reactions which occur between the flammable gases and the oxygen in the air, generate large amounts of energy. This energy causes a rise in the temperature of the gases produced in the reaction (the products of combustion) and also appears as thermal radiation (heat) and visible radiation (flame).

The high gas temperatures cause a vigorous upward movement driven by buoyancy; this induces mixing with the surrounding air by a process known as entrainment.

Low down in the plume, the centre will be rich in flammable gases and this will be surrounded by an envelope of flame.

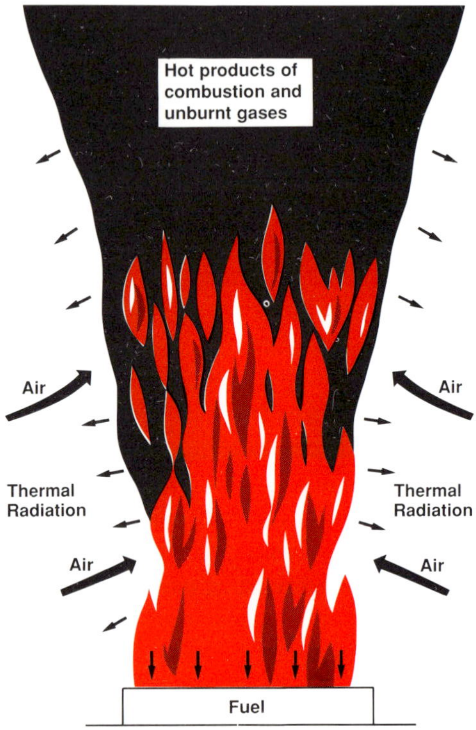

Figure 1.1 The Fire Plume

In the upper part of the plume, there is no flame. It is a rising column of smoke which consists of large amounts of entrained air, together with non-flammable products of combustion (mainly carbon dioxide and water), unburnt flammable gases and minute particles (soot). The flammable gases in the upper part of the fire are at too low a concentration to burn.

The upper part of the flame is basically unstable, producing the well-known flickering associated with fires. In general, though, the average flame height depends on the heat generated by the fire.

The hot plume radiates down on to the fuel, heating it, and so permitting the generation of flammable gases to continue. In general, there will be sufficient heat generated for the fire to spread as long as there is fuel nearby. However, during the early stages of a fire, it is not the main cause of fire spread. Nevertheless, the effect of thermal radiation can become more significant as the fire develops, as it is the cause of flashover. This is discussed later.

2 Fire Growth

Rapid fire spread occurs when the flames come into contact with new sources of fuel. This fuel will then be raised to very high temperatures, will itself start to generate flammable gases very quickly and eventually ignite. However, until the hot gases in the plume have been cooled by mixing with sufficient cool air, they will also be hot enough to cause fuel to start giving off flammable gases, if they come into contact with it.

Thermal radiation from the plume is the main element in fire spread wherever there is no direct flame impingement. Surrounding objects are heated until they in turn start to give off flammable gases.

The heat from the plume also heats up the air in the compartment as well as the walls, ceiling, floor and contents. As little as one third of the heat from a compartment fire will leave the compartment as hot smoke. As the compartment temperature rises, less and less heat from the plume can be absorbed by the compartment's walls and contents. The plume gets hotter and this increases the efficiency of the combustion process. It also further heats the fuel, increasing the rate at which the gases are generated. Thus, increasing compartment temperatures will result in increased combustion, as long as there is an adequate supply of oxygen.

3 The Effects of Water

Water is a most efficient firefighting agent. Apart from its ready availability in most parts of the country, and its cheapness, it has a couple of physical properties which work to the firefighter's advantage.

When any cold substance comes into contact with a hot one, heat is conducted from the hotter to the cooler. The important difference with cold water is that it gets changed from a liquid into a gas (steam) at 100°C. The amount of energy necessary to do this (the latent heat of vaporisation) is far higher than is necessary to heat water up to its boiling point. This energy has to come from somewhere. When water is turned into steam, large amounts of energy are absorbed from the hot gases and fuel in the fire, greatly cooling them.

When water is turned from a liquid into a gas, another very important physical effect occurs – it expands rapidly. If this were to happen in a sealed compartment this would cause a dangerous rise in pressure, but in a typical fire compartment, it causes a general outward flow of gases, driving the hot gases out of the compartment and preventing fresh air from reaching the fire. This can pose a hazard to firefighters due to the risk of burns from the hot gases and scalds from the steam.

These physical properties of water can be used to produce a wide variety of effects in a compartment fire. In some circumstances, the application of water can have a detrimental effect on firefighting but, properly applied:

- water directly cools the fuel to reduce further generation of flammable gases;

- water is converted into steam in the plume and the hot gases at ceiling level, absorbing heat, so cooling them and reducing the radiation heating the fuel;

- once converted into steam, water limits the amount of oxygen reaching the flames, smothering them;

- once converted into steam, water expands rapidly driving the products of combustion out of the compartment; and

- water cools the rest of the compartment, increasing the amount of heat it will absorb from the plume, so cooling it further.

4 The Effect of Walls and the Ceiling on the Plume

Combustion in the plume requires the presence of oxygen and the updraught from the plume draws air in towards it. If the fire is in the centre of the compartment, air will be drawn from all directions, although most will come from the direction of the primary air supply into the compartment.

If the fire is at a wall, the plume may attach itself to it. As air entrainment will only occur on one half of the plume, that half directly opposite the wall, it will take longer for the flammable gases to burn and the flame height will increase.

If the fire is in a corner, air entrainment can only occur over a quarter of the plume, so the flame will rise higher still. If the walls consist of flammable materials, and the plume contacts them, they will quickly become involved, further increasing the flame height.

When the plume reaches the ceiling, it will spread out, moving across the ceiling until it finds a way out. If it can't at first find a way out, the products of combustion will build up at ceiling level forming a smoke layer with, sometimes, a clearly defined boundary between it and clear air. This boundary closely matches the division between the cool gases at low level in the compartment, and the hot gases at ceiling level, which can be at a temperature of many hundreds of degrees Centigrade.

This boundary will descend as the fire grows. Once the products of combustion have found a way out, and the smoke supply from the plume matches the rate at which the smoke can leave the compartment, a degree of stability will result for a short while. The smoke boundary will stay roughly at the same height. This boundary could be lower than half the height of the compartment, depending on the layout of windows and doors, and the relative sizes of the compartment and the fire.

5 Actions by Firefighters

Firefighters should keep low in fires, to stay below this boundary. It must be remembered that the insulation in firefighters' clothing only serves to delay the time when they start to become uncomfortably hot and have to withdraw. If firefighters are to remain capable of working for any length of time inside a building on fire, they must avoid contact with hot gases whenever possible.

6 The Effect of Ventilation

The purpose of ventilation during a fire is to release the products of combustion from the compartment so as to prevent them causing further fire growth. Useful side effects of this are that, if the air-flows are properly managed, air temperatures will be reduced and visibility will be increased, making the firefighters' job easier. However, the firefighter should be aware that the increased air supply may cause the fire to intensify. This is discussed in more detail in the next section.

Ventilation is defined as:

> the planned and systematic removal of heated air, smoke, or other airborne contaminants from a structure and their replacement with a supply of fresher air.

The basic principles of ventilation are:

- whenever possible, hot gases should be released from high in the compartment, and the replacement fresh air should be allowed to enter at low level. This takes full advantage of the buoyancy of the hot gases, and minimises mixing within the compartment. The two vents should be similar in size;

- the high level vent should be down-wind of the low level vent, to take advantage of air flows induced by the wind;

- if it can be achieved, roof ventilation will be most effective and should be carried out as close to the fire as safety permits;

- the high level vent should be made before the low level vent;

- if possible, the compartment should be vented from outside the building. Any backdraught would then be directed outwards, with less risk to firefighters. The initial fireball might be spectacular, so the risk of igniting the building's eaves and surrounding risks would have to be considered, and charged branches made available to cover them; and

- the hot gases in the compartment can be cooled to reduce the potential for a backdraught, and the hot gases coming out of the vent can be cooled to prevent their ignition. Sprays and fogs have been found to be more effective than jets at this. However, water should not be directed in through the hot gas vent, as this may prevent the gases from escaping and drive fresh air in, inducing a backdraught.

Chapter 2
Backdraughts

1 Reducing the Oxygen Supply to a Fire

In general, the hot gases generated in the plume will rise extremely rapidly and will draw air in towards the fire. If there is an adequate air supply, the fire will continue to burn and grow as long as there is fuel available.

If the air supply to the compartment is restricted, the oxygen in the air inside may be used up more quickly than it can be replaced. The net effect will be a progressive lowering of the concentration of oxygen in the gases in the compartment, possibly combined with an increase in the temperature in the compartment.

As the oxygen concentration in the compartment reduces, the flames will start to die down, but this will not immediately result in a reduction in the production of flammable gases. Although the radiated heat from the plume reduces, the compartment is still very hot, and nothing has happened to cool the fuel. There may still be flames present, or they may die out altogether. Depending on the relative sizes of the fire and the compartment at this stage, sufficient flammable gases may be generated to spread throughout the compartment. This requires only a new supply of oxygen, caused for example by opening a door, for it to form an explosive mixture with potentially lethal consequences – a BACKDRAUGHT.

2 The Definition of a Backdraught

Limited ventilation can lead to a fire in a compartment producing fire gases containing significant proportions of partial combustion products and un-burnt pyrolysis products. If these accumulate then the admission of air when an opening is made to the compartment can lead to a sudden deflagration. This deflagration moving through the compartment and out of the opening is a **backdraught**

3 Possible Backdraught Scenarios

There are at least three different backdraught scenarios, any one of which could be awaiting the firefighter.

- If the fire is still burning in the compartment when the firefighter opens the door, and especially if the combustion gases are not escaping, the air which enters through the door may mix with the flammable gases, forming an explosive mixture.

If the gases in the compartment are hot enough, they will then ignite on their own (auto-ignite) at the doorway, and the flame will spread back into the compartment along with the fresh air supply. This would result in rapid fire growth, but not necessarily in a backdraught.

If the compartment gases are not that hot, they will be ignited when sufficient oxygen has reached the gases surrounding the fire. Flame will then travel across the compartment towards the door, resulting in flame shooting out of the door (Figure 2.1), driven by the expanding gases behind it. It is not easy to predict whether this will actually happen, or how long it will take, once the door has been opened. This will depend on where the fire is in the compartment, the rate at which air flows in through the door, and whether the hot gases can escape without mixing with the incoming air.

Figure 2.1 A Backdraught

● A more dangerous situation can occur when the fire in the compartment has almost died out. When the door is opened, the air flows in and an explosive mixture may be generated, but nothing happens because there is now no immediate source of ignition. If the firefighters now enter the compartment, their activities – for example, turning over – may expose a source of ignition, initiating a delayed backdraught but now with them inside the compartment and surrounded in flame (Figure 2.2).

This can still occur even when the fire is apparently out and the compartment has cooled down. If flammable gases remain in the compartment, they can be ignited. Cold smoke explosions occur in this way.

Figure 2.2 A Delayed Backdraught

● The situation can be further complicated if significant amounts of the flammable gases in the compartment have managed to escape into surrounding areas. Areas other than the closed compartment could then contain explosive atmospheres, waiting for a source of ignition. Most at risk is the area directly outside the compartment (Figure 2.3), exactly where the firefighters are waiting when they open the door. When the door is opened, a backdraught in the compartment would continue into other areas of the building. It is even possible, though unlikely, for other areas of the building to be involved in a backdraught, ignited without there being a backdraught in the original compartment. Flammable gases outside the compartment may be ignited by embers flying through the open door, or if the hot gases in the doorway auto-ignite.

Figure 2.3 A Backdraught Outside the Compartment

4 Signs and Symptoms of a Backdraught

The first clue to the possibility of a backdraught is the history of the fire: if the fire has been burning for some time, has generated lots of smoke which is now leaking out from the building, and has apparently died down without major areas of flame being visible from outside, the possibility is that it has died down from oxygen starvation.

When the building is viewed from outside, it is likely that the windows of the compartment concerned will be blackened with no obvious flames within. If part of a window is broken, it is possible that this will not provide sufficient oxygen to feed the fire. In this case it is likely that smoke will be pulsing out of the hole. Fresh air is drawn in as the fire cools slightly and the hot gases contract. This produces a local explosive mixture which burns, resulting in a mini-backdraught. The expansion of the hot gases in turn drives some smoke out of the compartment.

This cycle repeats itself at a frequency which depends on the size of the hole and the location of the fire relative to it.

If there is a gap under the compartment door, there may be smoke pulsing there due to the mini-backdraught effect already described. There may be a whistling noise if air is being drawn into the compartment through very small gaps around the door, but this could be difficult to hear. The door may be hot on the outside. In particular, the door handle may be hot if there is a metal rod linking it to the door handle on the other side.

If the compartment has been left long enough for it to cool down, air will no longer be drawn in, and the smoke pulsing effect will not be evident. However, if the compartment has not been ventilated and there are still flammable gases present, a backdraught is still possible.

If the decision is taken to open the door, there may be an in-rush of air as soon as the door is ajar, showing either that there is a shortage of oxygen in the compartment, or that the compartment has been much hotter and is starting to cool. Small flames may appear where the gases from the room are meeting the relatively fresh air outside, indicating that there are flammable gases in the room which are sufficiently hot to ignite given a source of fresh air, even without any other source of ignition. In either case, it may still be possible to close the door before sufficient air has entered the compartment to trigger any possible backdraught.

5 Actions by Firefighters

Once the door has been opened on to a compartment with an oxygen starved fire and fresh air has been allowed in, there is little which can be done to prevent a backdraught happening. It is far better to make appropriate decisions before the door is ever opened.

When firefighters are faced with a closed door, and do not know what is behind it, they should check for any of the signs and symptoms described above before opening it, covering the door with a charged branch, should they decide to open it. If there is a build-up of smoke outside the compartment, the possibility of backdraught can be reduced by spraying these gases before the compartment door is opened. The firefighters should be ready to close the door quickly, if a backdraught appears likely. This may not prevent the backdraught but may direct its force away from the firefighters.

If firefighters believe that opening a compartment door may lead to a backdraught, opening that door must be as a result of a deliberate decision. As long as the compartment door is closed, firefighters have time to think about their actions. Once the door is open, they will only have time to react to events as they occur. The decision on whether to *leave* this compartment until later is a responsibility that ultimately rests with the OIC of the incident.

However, the compartment will still have to be inspected at some stage. The priority is then to make it safe for the firefighters to enter. As already described, a backdraught can only occur when fresh air is permitted to enter the compartment. It is possible for firefighters to operate in a flammable atmosphere provided there is no opportunity for things to change and for fresh air to enter whilst the firefighters are inside. It is difficult to be sure – a window might shatter, someone might unwittingly open another door to the compartment. The far safer solution is to remove the flammable gases from the compartment – ventilation.

It is important to recognize that ventilation requires that fresh air should be let into the compartment. Thus, there is the possibility that a backdraught may occur during ventilation, so appropriate precautions should be taken.

If it is decided that a compartment needs to be ventilated and once the method of ventilation has been selected by the OIC of the incident:

- branches must be charged and in position prior to any ventilation being carried out;

- firefighters must get down low, and well clear of the likely flame path back through the vent opening, should a backdraught occur; and

- it must be remembered that a backdraught could be delayed several minutes and that it might have sufficient energy to break other windows in the compartment.

No compartment can be considered safe from a backdraught until it has been opened to fresh air for some time. However, once the compartment has been properly ventilated, firefighters can tackle the fire knowing that there is no longer any possibility of backdraught.

Chapter 3
Flashovers

1 Fire Spread

It has already been described in Chapter 1 Section 4 how a smoke layer will build up when smoke cannot escape from a compartment as quickly as it is generated (Figure 3.1). However, if there is unburnt fuel in the compartment, things will not stay stable for long. Initially, the flame in the plume will not reach the ceiling and fire spread will be limited to flammable materials close to the seat of the fire, ignited by radiated heat from the plume. Nevertheless, the fire is growing and the temperature in the compartment is rising, increasing the energy output from the plume.

Figure 3.1 The Build-up of the Smoke Layer

The flame height will increase until it reaches the ceiling. The flame will now start to spread across the compartment in the hot gas layer (Figure 3.2), with the flame appearing both at ceiling level above the plume, where air has been entrained, and at the boundary between the hot gas layer and clear air, as this is where the flammable gas in the ceiling layer can react with the oxygen.

Once flame has started to spread across the compartment at the boundary level, this will greatly increase the thermal radiation from the hot products of combustion already built up there. The other flammable materials in the compartment will now start to rise in temperature very rapidly. Not only are they being heated from the side by the plume, they are also being heated from above, where the flames and the hot products of combustion could be much closer, depending on the height of the boundary.

Figure 3.2 Flame in the Smoke Layer

In large compartments with higher ceilings, flame and the hot products of combustion may spread at ceiling level without getting low enough to cause nearby fuel sources to start giving off flammable gases.

However, it may be that, at some distance from the fire, either a discontinuity in the ceiling causes the hot gases to swirl lower, or there is a high pile of flammable material. In either of these cases, the source of thermal radiation has been brought closer to the fuel, and ignition may result. By this mechanism, fire spread can cut firefighters off from their means of escape.

As the hot smoke layer descends, and particularly if there is a low ceiling, all the remaining contents in the compartment will now be heated to the stage when they will themselves start to give off flammable gases (Figure 3.3). It is then only a matter of time before there is a sudden change in the size of the fire, if no action is taken to prevent it. The smaller the compartment, the sooner these conditions are likely to be encountered.

Figure 3.3 Rapid Heating of All Combustible Materials

Once flammable gases are being given off by the majority of the compartment contents, the transition from a localised fire to total involvement can take a matter of seconds –a FLASHOVER.

2 Definition of a Flashover

> In a compartment fire there can come a stage where the total thermal radiation from the fire plume, hot gases and hot compartment boundaries causes the radiative ignition of all exposed combustible surfaces within the compartment. This sudden and sustained transition of a growing fire to a fully developed fire is **flashover**.

It can be seen that, according to this definition, a backdraught can be a special case of a flashover. If the backdraught results in a *sustained* fully developed fire, a flashover has occurred. Nevertheless, it is important to be able to draw a distinction between the two because the implications for firefighters are very different.

3 Signs and Symptoms of a Flashover

The primary requirement for a flashover to occur is that there should be significant thermal radiation from above. This will be felt by the firefighters as a rapid increase in the temperature in the compartment, and in the heat from the hot gases at ceiling level, forcing them down low. If they can see above them, they will be able to see tongues of flame running through the gas layer. In addition, other combustible materials within the compartment will be giving off visible smoke, and flammable gases.

4 Actions by Firefighters

As the main reason for a flashover is radiation from the hot gases and flames above them, the logical solution is to cool this area. This will have the effect of reducing the flames and radiated heat, and causing the smoke layer to lift. Directing a spray at the ceiling will have this effect. However, too much water will cause the generation of large amounts of steam. Too much cooling will bring the smoke layer down, obscuring everything.

In these circumstances, it will be most effective for the firefighters to attack the hot gases with pulses of spray, observing their effect, and so judging when sufficient water has been applied.

Once the immediate danger of a flashover has been eliminated, the next steps depend on whether flashover conditions could re-develop before the fire can be extinguished. If this is likely, it is important to ventilate the fire as soon as possible.

If the hot gases are released faster than they are generated, the smoke layer will reduce, and the risk of flashover will reduce. Built-in roof vents are designed to do exactly this, either automatically, or when operated by the fire service. However, it is important that the correct vents are opened. The further from the fire that the vent is, the further the hot gases have to travel, and the more the chance of fire spread.

Where there are no built-in vents, firefighters have the option of making their own. It must be remembered, however, that incorrect use of ventilation can result in increased fire-spread at high level as hot gases are channelled into areas they might otherwise have taken longer to reach.

Chapter 4
Firefighter Awareness

Officers have the important responsibility of deciding whether to commit breathing apparatus teams inside a building. It is essential that they are aware of the potential for backdraughts and, where their occurrence is more likely, the outside of the building must be checked for indications of a possible backdraught, and appropriate warnings must be given to the crews before they are committed.

It is essential that, from the moment firefighters enter a building, they are constantly aware of the possibilities of backdraught and flashover, and that they stop, look and think before they open any door inside a building.

Bibliography

Drysdale, D. 1985 *An Introduction to Fire Dynamics*, John Wiley and Sons

Wharry, D. 1974 *Fire Technology – Chemistry and Combustion*, The Institution of Fire Engineers

Printed in the United Kingdom for HMSO
Dd 300508 C20 3/95 559 31887